SIMPLY SMART GRILL LUNCH

50 Delicious Recipes for Lunch using your Smart Grill

William Burn

© **Copyright 2021 - All rights reserved.**

The following Book is reproduced below to provide information that is as accurate and reliable as possible. Regardless, purchasing this Book can be seen as consent because both the Publisher and the author of this Book are in no way experts on the topics discussed within. Any recommendations or suggestions that are made herein are for entertainment purposes only. Professionals should be consulted as needed before undertaking any of the actions endorsed herein.

This declaration is deemed fair and valid by both the American Bar Association and the Publishers Association Committee. It is legally binding throughout the United States.

Furthermore, the transmission, duplication, or reproduction of any of the following work, including specific information, will be considered an illegal act irrespective of if it is done electronically or in print. This extends to creating a secondary or tertiary copy of the work or a recorded copy and is only allowed with the Publisher's express written consent. All additional rights reserved.

The information in the following pages is broadly considered a truthful and accurate account of facts. As such, any inattention, use, or misuse of the information in question by the reader will render any resulting actions solely under their purview. There are no scenarios in which the Publisher or the original author of this work can be in any fashion deemed liable for any hardship or damages that may befall them after undertaking the information described herein.

Additionally, the information in the following pages is intended only for informational purposes. It should thus be thought of as universal. As befitting its nature, it is presented without assurance regarding its prolonged validity or interim quality. Trademarks that are mentioned are done without written consent and can in no way be considered an endorsement from the trademark holder.

Chapter 1: Breakfast recipes

1. Zucchini Pancakes

Preparation time: 10 minutes

Cooking time: 10 minutes

Servings: 6

Ingredients:

- 1 cup almond milk, unsweetened 1 egg

- 2 tbsp. honey

- 1 tbsp. coconut oil melted 1 tsp. vanilla

- ½ cup zucchini, grated

- 1 ½ cup oat flour

- 2 tsp. cinnamon

- 1 tsp. baking powder

- ¼ tsp. salt

- Nonstick cooking spray

Directions:

1. In a large bowl, combine milk, egg, honey, oil, vanilla, and zucchini.

2. In a separate bowl, stir together the remaining ingredients. Add to zucchini mixture and mix just until combined.

3. Spray the cooking pot with cooking spray. Set to sauté on medium heat.

4. Pour batter, ¼ cup at a time, into the cooking pot. Cook 3-4 minutes or until bubble form in the middle. Flip and cook for another 2-3 minutes. Repeat with the remaining batter. Serve immediately with your favorite toppings.

Nutrition: Calories: 188, Total Fat: 7 g, Total Carbs: 27 g, Net Carbs: 25 g, Protein: 6 g, Sugar: 8 g, Sodium: 132 mg, Potassium: 258 mg, Phosphorus: 227 mg.

2. Juicy Mushroom Frittata

Preparation time: 10 minutes

Cooking time: 10 minutes

Servings: 1

Ingredients:

- 4 cremini mushrooms, sliced

- ½ cup cheddar cheese, shredded

- 4 large eggs

- ¼ cup whole milk

- ½ bell pepper, seeded and diced

- ½ onion, chopped

- Salt and pepper, to taste

Directions:

1. Add the whisked egg, milk, salt, and pepper into a medium-sized bowl

2. Add bell pepper, mushroom, cheese, and onion

3. Mix them well

4. Preheat your Smart Grill XL by pressing the "Bake" mode at 400 °F

5. Set the timer for 10 minutes

6. Let it preheat until you hear a beep

7. Pour the egg mixture into your Smart Grill Bake pan

8. Spread the mixture evenly

9. Transfer to Grill and lock the lid

10. Bake for 10 minutes

11. Once cooked, serve

12. Enjoy!

Nutrition: Calories: 153, Fat: 1 g, Saturated Fat: 0 g, Carbs: 5 g, Fiber: 2 g, Sodium: 245 mg, Protein: 11 g.

3. **French Morning Toasties**

Preparation time: 5-10 minutes

Cooking time: 10 minutes

Servings: 4

Ingredients:

- Cooking spray as needed

- 6 slices bread, sliced into strips

- ¼ tsp. vanilla extract

- ¼ tsp. ground cinnamon

- ¼ cup Granulated Sugar:

- ½ cup milk

- 4 whole eggs

Directions:

1. Take a bowl and beat in eggs, milk

2. Stir in sugar, vanilla, and cinnamon

3. Dip the bread in the mix

4. Preheat your Smart Grill Smart XL in Air Crisp for 10 minutes at 400 °F

5. Transfer bread to the Foodi and cook for 3-5 minutes per side

6. Enjoy!

Nutrition: Calories: 183, Fat: 6 g, Saturated Fat: 2 g, Carbs: 24 g, Fiber: 3 g, Sodium: 269 mg, Protein: 9 g.

4. <u>Delicious Mac and Cheese</u>

Preparation time: 5-10 minutes

Cooking time: 10 minutes

Servings: 4

Ingredients:

- 1 tbsp. parmesan cheese, grated

- 1 cup elbow macaroni

- One and ½ cheddar cheese, grated

- ½ cup broccoli

- 1 cup milk, warmed

- Salt and pepper, to taste

Directions:

1. Preheat your Smart Grill XL by pressing the "Air Crisp" option and setting it to 400 °F

2. Set the timer to 10 minutes

3. Let it preheat until you hear a beep

4. Take a pot and add water

5. Allow it to boil

6. Add macaroni and veggies and boil for 10 minutes

7. Drain the pasta and vegetable using a colander

8. Add cheese to the pasta and vegetable mixture

9. Toss them well

10. Season with Salt and pepper

11. Transfer the mixture to your Foodi

12. Sprinkle some more parmesan on top

13. Cook for about 15 minutes

14. Let it cool for 10 minutes

15. Serve and enjoy!

Nutrition: Calories: 180, Fat: 11 g, Saturated Fat: 3 g, Carbs: 14 g, Fiber: 3 g, Sodium: 287 mg, Protein: 9 g.

Chapter 2: Delicious Snack & Appetizer Recipes

5. <u>Grilled Fruit Skewers</u>

Preparation time: 20 minutes

Cooking time: 12 minutes

Servings: 12

Ingredients:

- 8 peaches, sliced

- 1½ pints strawberries, sliced

- 1½ cups pineapples, cut into large cubes

- 3 tbsp. honey

- Salt, to taste

- 3 tbsp. olive oil

- 10 skewers, soaked in water for 20 minutes

Directions:

1. Select the "Grill" button on the Smart Grill Smart XL Grill and regulate Medium settings for 12 minutes.

2. Insert the strawberries, pineapples, and peaches on the skewers.

3. Dust with Salt and shower with olive oil.

4. Arrange the skewers inside the Smart Grill when it displays "Add Food."

5. Grill for 12 minutes, turning twice in between.

6. Trickle the grilled fruits with honey and serve well.

Nutrition: Calories: 132, Fat: 4.7g, Sat Fat: 0.6g, Carbs: 23.8 g.

6. <u>Cute Mozarella Bites</u>

Preparation time: 5-10 minutes

Cooking time: 8 minutes

Servings: 12

Ingredients:

- 1 cup breadcrumbs

- ¼ cup butter, melted

- 12 mozzarella strips

Directions:

1. Dip the mozzarella strips in butter

2. Dredge them with breadcrumbs

3. Add mozzarella strips to your Smart Grill Smart XL Crisping basket

4. Cook at 320 °F for 8 minutes on Air Crisp mode

5. Cook for 8 minutes, making sure to flip once

6. Serve and enjoy!

Nutrition: Calories: 206, Fat: 12 g, Saturated Fat: 5 g, Carbs: 16 g, Fiber: 5 g, Sodium: 284 mg, Protein: 10 g.

7. S'mores Roll-Up

Preparation time: 10 minutes

Cooking time: 5 minutes

Servings: 2

Ingredients:

- 4 graham crackers

- 2 cups mini marshmallows

- 2 flour tortillas

- 2 cups chocolate chips

Directions:

1. Select the "Grill" button on the Smart Grill Smart XL Grill and regulate Medium settings for 5 minutes.

2. Split the graham crackers, chocolate chips, and marshmallows on the tortillas.

3. Tightly wrap up the tortillas and arrange them inside the Smart Grill when it displays "Add Food."

4. Grill for 5 minutes, flipping once in between.

5. Dole out on a plate when completely grilled to serve.

Nutrition: Calories: 429, Fat: 13.6 g, Sat Fat: 6 g, Carbs: 72.7 g, Fiber: 3.3 g, Sugar: 57.8 g, Protein: 5.9 g.

8. Original Crispy Tomatoes

Preparation time: 5-10 minutes

Cooking time: 5 minutes

Servings: 4

Ingredients:

- Breadcrumbs as needed

- ½ cup buttermilk

- ¼ cup almond flour

- Salt and pepper to taste

- ¼ tbsp. Creole seasoning

- 1 green tomato

Directions:

1. Preheat Smart Grill Smart XL by pressing the "Air Crisp" option and setting it to "400 °F" and timer to 5 minutes

2. Let it preheat until you hear a beep

3. Add flour to your plate and take another plate and add buttermilk

4. Cut tomatoes and season with Salt and pepper

5. Make a mix of creole seasoning and crumbs

6. Take tomato slice and cover with flour, place in buttermilk and then into crumbs

7. Repeat with all tomatoes

8. Cook the tomato slices for 5 minutes

9. Serve with basil and enjoy!

Nutrition: Calories: 200, Fat: 12 g, Saturated Fat: 4 g, Carbs: 11 g, Fiber: 2 g, Sodium: 1203 mg, Protein: 3 g.

Chapter 3: Chicken Recipes

9. __Turkey Croquettes__

Preparation time: 10 minutes

Cooking time: 20 minutes

Servings: 10

Ingredients:

- Nonstick cooking spray

- 2 ½ cups turkey, cooked

- 1 stalk celery, chopped

- 2 green onions, chopped

- ½ cup cauliflower, cooked

- ½ cup broccoli, cooked

- 1 cup stuffing, cooked

- 1 cup cracker crumbs

- 1 egg, lightly beaten

- 1/8 tsp. salt

- 1/8 tsp. pepper

- 1 cup French fried onions crushed

Directions:

1. Spray the fryer basket with cooking spray.

2. Add the turkey, celery, onion, cauliflower, and broccoli to a food processor and pulse until finely chopped. Transfer to a large bowl.

3. Stir in stuffing and 1 cup of the cracker crumbs until combined.

4. Add the egg, salt, and pepper and stir to combine. Form into 10 patties.

5. Place the crushed fried onions in a shallow dish. Coat patties on both sides in the onions and place in the basket. Lightly spray the tops with cooking spray.

6. Add the tender-crisp lid and set it to air fry on 375 °F. Cook 5-7 minutes until golden brown. Flip over and spray with cooking spray again; cook another 5-7 minutes. Serve immediately.

Nutrition: Calories: 133, Total Fat: 4 g, Total Carbs: 16 g, Net Carbs: 15 g, Protein: 9 g, Sugar: 1 g, Sodium: 449 mg, Potassium: 136 mg, Phosphorus: 85 mg.

10. <u>Southern-Style Chicken</u>

Preparation time: 5 minutes

Cooking time: 20 minutes

Servings: 6

Ingredients:

- 2 cups Ritz crackers, crushed

- 1 tbsp. fresh parsley, minced

- 1 tsp. garlic salt

- ¼ tsp. rubbed sage

- 1 tsp. paprika

- 1 large egg, beaten

- ½ tsp. black pepper

- 1 (3-4 pounds) broiler/fryer chicken, cut up

- ¼ tsp. ground cumin

Directions:

2. Select the "Air Crisp" button on the Smart Grill Smart XL Grill and regulate the settings at 350 °F for 20 minutes.

3. Whip the egg in a bowl and mingle the rest of the ingredients except chicken in another bowl.

4. Immerse the chicken in the whipped egg and then dredge in the dry mixture.

5. Arrange the chicken in the Smart Grill when it displays "Add Food."

6. Air Crisp for about 20 minutes and dole out to serve warm.

Nutrition: Calories: 391, Fat: 2.8 g, Sat Fat: 0.6 g, Carbs: 16.5 g, Fiber: 9.2 g, Sugar: 4.2 g, Protein: 26.6 g.

11. Clean Apple Flavored Alfredo Chicken

Preparation time: 5-10 minutes

Cooking time: 20 minutes

Servings: 4

Ingredients:

- 1 large apple, wedged

- 1 tbsp. lemon juice

- 4 chicken breasts, halved

- 4 tsp. s chicken seasoning

- 4 slices provolone cheese

- ¼ cup blue cheese, crumbled

- ½ cup Alfredo sauce

Directions:

2. Take a mixing bowl and add seasoning

3. Take another bowl and toss the apple with lemon juice

4. Set your Smart Grill Smart XL to Grill and medium mode, set timer to 16 minutes

5. Transfer chicken over grill grate, lock lid and cook for 8 minutes

32

6. Flip and cook for 8 minutes more

7. Grill the apple in a similar manner, 2 minutes per side

8. Serve the cooked chicken with sauce, grilled apple, and cheese

9. Enjoy!

Nutrition: Calories: 247, Fat: 19 g, Saturated Fat: 3 g, Carbs: 29 g, Fiber: 2 g, Sodium: 850 mg, Protein: 14 g.

Chapter 4: Beef, Pork & Lamb Recipes

12. <u>Simple Lamb Chop</u>

Preparation time: 5 minutes

Cooking time: 25 minutes

Servings: 2

Ingredients:

- 2 medium lamb chops

- 1 tbsp. lemon juice

- 1 tsp. dried rosemary

- 1 tsp. dried thyme

- Salt and pepper to taste

Directions:

2. Preheat the Air Fryer to 350 °F.

3. Combine all the ingredients to season the lamb chops thoroughly.

4. Place the lamb chops in the air fryer basket for 25 minutes.

5. Allow the lamb chops to rest for 10 minutes before serving.

Nutrition: Calories: 265, Carbs: 5.9 g, Fat: 15.2 g, Protein: 25.2 g.

13. Herbed Rack of Lamb

Preparation time: 7 minutes

Cooking time: 10 minutes

Servings: 4

Ingredients:

- 1 rack of lamb

- 3 tbsp. olive oil

- 1 tbsp. dried rosemary

- 1 tbsp. dried thyme

- 2 garlic cloves, minced

- Salt and pepper to taste

Directions:

2. Preheat the air fryer to 360 °F.

3. Combine all the ingredients except the rack of lamb in a small bowl to form the seasoning.

4. Rub the mixture all over the rack of lamb and place the rack of lamb into the air fryer basket. Cook for 10 minutes and check the internal temperature. For rare meat, the internal temperature should be 145 °F. For medium meat,

the internal temperature should be 160 °F. For well-done meat, the internal temperature should be 170 °F.

5. Serve with your favorite sides after the lamb has rested for a minimum of 10 minutes.

Nutrition: Calories: 287, Carbs: 1.5 g, Fat: 20.7 g, Protein: 23.2 g.

14. <u>Leg of Lamb</u>

Preparation   **time:**   5   minutes

Cooking   **time:**   40   minutes

Servings: 5

Ingredients:

- 1 leg of lamb

- Salt and pepper to taste

Directions:

2. Preheat the air fryer to 360 °F.

3. Season the leg of lamb with Salt and pepper, then place in the air fryer basket. Cook for 40 minutes.

4. Serve warm with desired sides

Nutrition: Calories: 243, Carbs: 0 g, Fat: 9.6 g, Protein: 36 g.

Chapter 5: Roasted Recipes

15. Crispy Crunchy Broccoli Delight

Preparation time: 5-10 minutes

Cooking time: 15 minutes

Servings: 3

Ingredients:

- Lemon wedges

- 2 tbsp. parmesan, grated

- Salt and pepper to taste

- 2 tbsp. extra virgin olive oil

- 1 large broccoli head, cut into florets

- ¼ cup toasted almonds, sliced

- ½ tsp. red pepper flakes

Directions:

1. Take a medium bowl and add broccoli, toss with olive oil

2. Season well with Salt and pepper

3. Add pepper flakes for heat

4. Preheat your Smart Grill Grill in Air Crisp mode to 390 °F, and set the timer to 15 minutes

5. Once you hear the beep, arrange a reversible trivet in Grill Pan

6. Arrange broccoli and roast until the timer is out

7. Serve with some cheese on top and the lemon wedges on the side

8. *Enjoy!*

Nutrition: Calories: 181, Fat: 11 g, Saturated Fat: 3 g, Carbs: 9 g, Fiber: 4 g, Sodium: 421 mg, Protein: 8 g.

Chapter 6: Fried Recipes

16. Delicious Avocado Chips

Preparation time: 10 minutes

Cooking time: 10 minutes

Servings: 4

Ingredients:

- 4 tbsp. butter

- 4 raw avocados, peeled and sliced in chips

- Salt and pepper to taste

Directions:

1. Season avocado slices with salt and pepper

2. Grease pot of Smart Grill with butter and add the avocado slices

3. Air Crisp for 10 minutes at 350 °F

4. Remove from Foodi and transfer to a plate

5. Serve and enjoy!

Nutrition: Calories: 391, Fat: 38 g, Saturated Fat: 8 g, Carbs: 15 g, Fiber: 3 g, Sodium: 450 mg, Protein: 3.5 g.

Chapter 7: Baked Recipes

17. Baked Parmesan Fish

Preparation time: 5-10 minutes

Cooking time: 13 minutes

Servings: 3

Ingredients:

- ¼ tsp. salt

- ¾ cup breadcrumbs

- ¼ cup parmesan cheese, grated

- ¼ tsp. ground dried thyme

- ¼ cup butter, melted

- 1-pound haddock fillets

- ¾ cup milk

Directions:

1. Coat fish fillets in milk, season with salt and keep it on the side

2. Take a mixing bowl and add breadcrumbs, parmesan, cheese, thyme, and combine well

3. Coat fillets in bread crumb mixture

4. Preheat Smart Grill by pressing the "Bake" option and setting it to "325 °F" and timer to 13 minutes

5. Let it preheat until you hear a beep

6. Arrange fish fillets directly over Grill Grate, lock lid and cook for 8 minutes, flip and cook for the remaining time

7. Serve and enjoy!

Nutrition: Calories: 450, Fat: 27 g, Saturated Fat: 12 g, Carbs: 16 g, Fiber: 22 g, Sodium: 1056 mg, Protein: 44 g.

18. Chocolate Cheesecake

Preparation time: 15 minutes

Cooking time: 15 minutes

Servings: 6

Ingredients:

- 2 cups cream cheese, softened

- 2 eggs

- 2 tbsp. cocoa powder

- 1 tsp. pure vanilla extract

- ½ cup Swerve

Directions:

- Add eggs, cocoa powder, vanilla extract, swerve, cream cheese in an immersion blender and blend until smooth.

- Pour the mixture evenly into mason jars.

- Put the mason jars in the insert of Smart Grill and close the lid.

- Select "Bake/Roast" and bake for 15 minutes at 360 °F.

- Refrigerate for at least 2 hours.

Nutrition: Calories: 244, Total Fat: 24.8 g, Saturated Fat 15.6 g, Cholesterol 32 mg, Sodium: 204 mg, Total Carbs: 2.1 g, Fiber 0.1 g, Sugar: 0.4 g, Protein: 4 g.

Chapter 8: Grilled Recipes

19. Easy Grilled Pork Chops with Sweet & Tangy Mustard Glaze

Preparation time: 10 minutes

Cooking time: 45 minutes

Servings: 4

Ingredients:

For the Glace:

- 1 ½ tsp. cider

- 1 tsp. Dijon mustard

- 2 tsp. brown sugar

For the Brine:

- 3 cups light brown

- 2 bay leaves

- 2 tsp. of salt

- 2 cloves smashed

- 1 ½ cups of ice cubes

- 4 boneless pork chops

Directions:

1. Make the glaze by placing the ingredients in a small bowl and set them aside.

2. Brine your pork by placing it inside the water with bay leaves, brown sugar, and garlic and heat it on medium heat. Cover and bring the mixture to a boil. Uncover and stir it until the Sugar: is completely dissolved in the mixture. Add ice cubes to cool into; it is slightly warm to the touch.

3. Once it is cooled, submerge the pork chops and set aside for 15 minutes. Prepare your grill. Put the Instant Smart Grill fryer on Grill mode and wait for it to attain the desired temperature. Once it has attained 400 ° C, then it is time to add your pork chops. Usually, the appliance will be indicated 'add food.'

4. Remove the pork chops from the salt mixture and pat them with paper towels. Place them on the grill and cover. Do not remove until they are well cooked once the instant fryer indicates Turn Food. Flip your food and glaze it twice before allowing it to cook some more.

5. Transfer the pork to a clean cutting board once the appliance has indicated an end. Serve while hot.

Nutrition: Calories: 355.9, Fat 20.7 g, Carbs 21.2 g, Fiber 0.3%, Protein: 21.2 g.

20. Spiced Up Grilled Shrimp

Preparation time: 5-10 minutes

Cooking time: 6 minutes

Servings: 4

Ingredients:

- 2 tbsp. brown sugar:

- 1 pound jumbo shrimp, peeled and deveined

- 2 tbsp. olive oil

- 1 tbsp. garlic powder

- 1 tbsp. paprika

- ½ tsp. black pepper

- 1 tsp. garlic salt

Directions:

1. Take a bowl and add listed ingredients gently mix

2. Let the mixture chill for 30-60 minutes

3. Preheat your Grill in Medium mode setting the timer to 6 minutes

4. Once you hear the beep, arrange your prepared shrimp over the grill grate

5. Lock and let it cook for 3 minutes

6. Flip and cook for 3 minutes more

7. Once done, serve and enjoy!

Nutrition: Calories: 370, Fat: 27 g, Saturated Fat: 3 g, Carbs: 23 g, Fiber: 8 g, Sodium: 182 mg, Protein: 6 g.

Chapter 9: Fish and Seafood Recipes

21. Spiced Tilapia

Preparation time: 10 minutes

Cooking time: 12 minutes

Servings: 2

Ingredients:

- ½ tsp. lemon-pepper seasoning

- ½ tsp. garlic powder

- 1/2 tsp. onion powder

- Salt and freshly ground black pepper, to taste

- 2 (6-ounces) tilapia fillets

- 1 tbsp. olive oil

Directions:

1. In a small bowl, mix the spices, salt, and black pepper.

2. Coat the tilapia fillets with oil and then rub with spice mixture.

3. Arrange the greased "Crisper Basket" in the pot of Smart Grill Grill.

4. Close the Smart Grill Grill with lid and *select* "Air Crisp."

5. Set the temperature to 360 °F to preheat.

6. Press "Start/Stop" to begin preheating.

7. When the display shows "Add Food," open the lid and place the tilapia fillets into the "Crisper Basket."

8. Close the Smart Grill with a lid and *set the time* for 12 minutes.

9. Press "Start/Stop" to begin cooking.

10. Flip the fillets once halfway through.

11. When the Cook time is completed, press "Start/Stop" to stop cooking and open the lid.

12. Serve hot.

Nutrition: Calories: 206, Fat: 8.6 g, Saturated Fat: 1.7 g, Carbs: 1.3 g, Sugar: 0.4 g, Protein: 31.9 g.

22. Perfect Grilled Mahi-Mahi

Preparation time: 10 minutes

Cooking time: 20 minutes

Servings: 2

Ingredients:

- 3 mahi-mahi fillets

- 2 tbsp. fresh lemon juice

- 1 tsp. cumin

- 1 tsp. dried oregano

- 1/8 tsp. cayenne pepper

- ½ tsp. onion powder

- ½ tsp. garlic powder

- 1 tsp. paprika

- 3 tbsp. olive oil

- ¼ tsp. pepper

- ½ tsp. salt

Directions:

1. In a small bowl, mix cumin, oregano, cayenne, garlic powder, paprika, pepper, and salt.

2. Brush fish fillets with oil and season with spice mixture.

3. Place the cooking pot in the unit, then place the grill grate in the pot and close the hood.

4. Select grill mode then set the temperature to medium and set the timer to 10 minutes. Press start to begin preheating.

5. Once the unit is preheated, it will then beep then place fish fillets on grill grates and close the hood.

6. Cook fish fillets for 5 minutes, then flip fish fillets and continue cooking for 5 minutes.

7. Drizzle fish fillets with lemon juice and serve.

Nutrition: Calories: 162, Fat 14.4 g, Carbs: 2.1 g, Sugar: 0.6 g, Protein: 7.5 g, Cholesterol 13 mg.

23. Old Bay Seasoned Shrimp

Preparation time: 10 minutes

Cooking time: 20 minutes

Servings: 2

Ingredients:

- 1/2 lb. shrimp, peeled and deveined

- 1/2 tsp. old bay seasoning

- 1/2 tsp. cayenne pepper

- 1 tbsp. olive oil

- 1/4 tsp. paprika

- Pinch of salt

Directions:

1. Add shrimp and remaining ingredients into the mixing bowl and toss well to coat.

2. Place the cooking pot in the unit, then place the crisper basket in the pot and close the hood.

3. Select Air Crisp mode, then set the temperature to 390 °F and set the timer to 6 minutes. Press start to begin preheating.

4. Once the unit is preheated, it will beep then place shrimp in the basket. Close the hood.

5. Cook shrimp for 6 minutes.

6. Serve and enjoy.

Nutrition: Calories: 195, Fat 9 g, Carbs: 2 g, Sugar: 0.1 g, Protein: 26 g, Cholesterol 239 mg.

Chapter 10: Dehydrated Recipes

24. Fried Pickles

Preparation time: 15 minutes

Cooking time: 3 minutes

Servings: 6

Ingredients:

- 36 cold dill pickle slices

- 2 tbsp. chopped fresh dill

- 1 tsp. salt

- 1 cup divided cornstarch

Ranch Dressing:

- ¼ tsp. cayenne

- 2 tsp. black pepper

- ½ cup almond meal

- 1 large egg

- ¾ cup almond milk

- 2 tsp. paprika

- Canola oil

Directions:

70

1. Whisk together cayenne, milk, and egg.

2. Spread half-cup cornstarch in a shallow dish.

3. Mix the remaining ½-cup cornstarch with almond meal, salt, pepper, dill, and paprika.

4. Dredge the pickle slices first through the cornstarch, then dip them in egg wash.

5. Coat them with the almond meal mixture and shake off the excess.

6. Place them in the fryer basket and spray them with oil.

Return the basket to the fryer and air fry the pickles for 3 minutes at 3700 F, working in batches to not crowd the basket.

7. Serve warm.

Nutrition: Calories: 138, Fat: 12.2 g. Carbs: 5.8 g. Protein: 4 g.

Chapter 11: Tasty Dessert Recipe

25. Corn Bread

Preparation time: 5 minutes

Cooking time: 25 minutes

Servings: 4

Ingredients:

- 2 eggs

- ½ tsp. kosher salt

- ½ cup yellow cornmeal

- 1 ½ tsp. baking powder

- 1/2 cup all-purpose flour

- Fresh corn kernels

- ½ cup whole milk

- ¼ cup vegetable oil

- 2 tbsp. sugar

Directions:

1. Set all the dry ingredients in a medium bowl and whisk.

2. In another bowl, put in all the wet ingredients. Gently mix until combined. Gradually add the dry mixture into the

bowl. Mix until smooth. Add the corn and mix until combined.

3. Spread the mixture into a greased baking tray. Put it in the cooking basket — Cook for 25 minutes at 350 °F.

4. Slice after cooling down, then serve.

Nutrition: Calories: 372, Fat: 20.16 g, Carbs: 39.04 g, Protein: 8.87 g.

Chapter 9: Fish and Seafood Recipes

26. Banana Chips

Preparation time: 10 minutes

Cooking time: 15 minutes

Servings: 4

Ingredients:

- Chat masala, ½ tsp.

- Turmeric powder, ½ tsp.

- Olive oil, 1 tsp.

- Peeled and sliced bananas, 4.

- Salt, ¼ tsp.

Directions:

1. In a bowl, mix banana slices with oil, chaat masala, turmeric, and salt. Toss and set aside for 10 minutes.

2. Allow cooking in the air fryer at 360 °F for 15 minutes. Flip them once.

3. Serve.

Nutrition: Calories: 121, Fat: 1 g, Protein: 3 g, Carbs: 3 g.

27. Choco-Peanut Mug Cake

Preparation time: 5 minutes

Cooking time: 20 minutes

Servings: 1

Ingredients:

- 1 tsp. softened butter

- 1 egg

- 1 tbsp. peanut butter

- ½ tsp. vanilla extract

- 2 tbsp. Erythritol

- 2 tbsp. unsweetened cocoa powder

- ¼ tsp. baking powder

- 1 tbsp. heavy cream

Directions:

1. Preheat the air fryer for 5 minutes.

2. Combine all ingredients in a mixing bowl.

3. Pour into a greased mug.

4. Set in the air fryer basket and cook for 20 minutes at 400 °F

Nutrition: Calories: 293, Protein: 12.4 g, Fat: 23.3 g, Carbs: 8.5 g.

28. Raspberry-Coco Desert

Preparation time: 5 minutes

Cooking time: 20 minutes

Servings: 12

Ingredients:

- 1 tsp. vanilla bean

- 1 cup pulsed raspberries

- 1 cup coconut milk

- 3 cup desiccated coconut

- ¼ cup coconut oil

- 1/3 cup Erythritol powder

Directions:

1. Preheat the air fryer for 5 minutes.

2. Combine all ingredients in a mixing bowl.

3. Pour into a greased baking dish.

4. Bake in the air fryer for 20 minutes at 375 °F.

Nutrition: Calories: 132, Carbs: 9.7 g, Fat: 9.7 g, Protein: 1.5 g.

29. Almond Cherry Bars

Preparation time: 5 minutes

Cooking time: 35 minutes

Servings: 12

Ingredients:

- 1 tbsp. Xanthan gum

- 1 ½ cup almond flour

- ½ tsp. salt

- 1 cup pitted fresh cherries

- ½ cup softened butter

- 2 eggs

- ¼ cup water

- ½ tsp. vanilla

- 1 cup Erythritol

Directions:

1. Combine almond flour, softened butter, salt, vanilla, eggs, and Erythritol in a large bowl until you form a dough.

2. Press the dough in a baking dish that will fit in the air fryer.

3. Set in the air fryer and bake for 10 minutes at 3750F

4. Meanwhile, mix the cherries, water, and xanthan gum in a bowl.

5. Take the dough out and pour over the cherry mixture.

6. Cook again for 25 minutes more at 375 °F in the air fryer.

Nutrition: Calories: 99, Carbs: 2.1 g, Fat: 9.3 g, Protein: 1.8 g.

BONUS: Original Exclusive Creative Recipes for Advanced Users

1. Sauteed Cauliflower Delight

Preparation time: 15 minutes

Cooking time: 30 minutes

Servings: 4

Ingredients:

- 1 red onion, to be chopped

- 1 cup of cherry tomatoes

- 1 tsp. of white sugar

- ¼ cup of olive oil

- 1 head of cauliflower, to be cut into florets

- 2 tbsp. of raisins

- 1 clove of garlic, to be minced

- ¼ tsp. of red pepper flakes

- 1 tsp. of dried parsley

- 1 tbsp. of fresh lemon juice

Directions:

1. Put the olive oil in a large skillet and heat over medium heat. Cook and stir the onion until it becomes tender in

about 5 to 10 minutes. Add cherry tomatoes, cauliflower, raisins, onion, and white sugar, cover the skillet, and cook while frequently stirring until the cauliflower becomes tender in about 4 to 5 minutes.

2. Mix the parsley, garlic, and red pepper flakes inside the cauliflower mixture. Increase the heat to high and sauté until the cauliflower becomes brown in about 1-2 minutes — drizzle lemon juice over the cauliflower.

Nutrition: Calories: 196.5, Carbs: 17.8 g, Protein: 3.7 g, Fat 13.9 g, Sodium: 49.2 mg.

2. <u>Brown Rice Stir-Fry with Vegetables</u>

Preparation time: 10 minutes

Cooking time: 45 minutes

Servings: 2 to 4

Ingredients:

- 1 cup (80 g) of chopped cabbage

- ½ cup (100 g) of uncooked brown rice

- ½ chopped red bell pepper

- ½ head of chopped broccoli

- 2 tbsp. of extra virgin olive oil

- ½ cup of chopped zucchini

- 1 handful of fresh parsley should be finely chopped

- 4 cloves of minced garlic

- 2 tbsp. of tamari or soy sauce

- 1 /8 tsp. of cayenne powder

- Sesame seeds for garnishing (optional)

Directions:

1. Check the direction on the brown rice and cook as directed

86

2. Put some water in a frying pan or wok and let it boil. After it boils, add the veggies (note that the water must cover these veggies) and cook for about 1-2 minutes on high heat. Drain the veggies and put them aside.

3. Heat the oil in the wok and add cayenne powder, parsley, and garlic. Cook with high heat for 1-minute, stirring frequently.

4. Add the rice, vegetables, and tamari — Cook for 1-2 minutes or more.

5. Add some sesame seeds if you like for garnishing (optional)

6. Store the brown rice stir-fry in a sealed container in the fridge for about 5 days.

Nutrition: Calories: 197, Protein: 5.6 g, Carbohydrates: 28.1 g, Fat: 7.9 g, Saturated Fat: 1.1 g, of Sugar: 3.5 g, Fiber: 4.1 g, Sodium: 476.8 mg.

3. __Broccoli and Cheese Calzone__

Preparation time: 15 minutes

Cooking time: 35 minutes

Servings: 4

Ingredients:

- 8 ounces of shredded part-skim mozzarella cheese

- Black pepper

- Salt

- 1 (15-ounces) container of part-skim ricotta cheese

- 1 (10-ounces) package broccoli florets, to be thawed and drained

- 2 tbsp. of grated parmesan

- 1 pound of bread or pizza dough, to be thawed

Directions:

1. Get a medium bowl, then combine mozzarella, ricotta, and broccoli. Mix very well. Then season with black pepper and salt

2. Roll dough to a 12-inches circle. Spread the cheese to fill 1 side of the circle to about a 1-inch edge. Lift 1 side of the dough and fold over in another to meet the other side

and form a half-moon and pinch the edges together to create a seal.

3. Preheat the oven to about 4000F.

4. Transfer the calzone to a large baking sheet and sprinkle it with cheese. Bake for 15 minutes until it becomes golden brown. Allow it to stand for 15 minutes before you slice.

Nutrition: Calories: 207.2, Carbs: 17 g, Protein: 9.2 g, Fat: 12.4 g, Cholesterol: 31.9 mg, Sodium: 528 mg.

4. Roasted Spicy Potatoes

Preparation time: 15 minutes

Cooking time: 25 minutes

Servings: 4

Ingredients:

- 1 lb. baby potatoes, sliced into wedges

- 2 tbsp. olive oil

- Salt to taste

- 1 tbsp. garlic powder

- 1 tbsp. paprika

- ½ cup mayonnaise

- 2 tbsp. white wine vinegar

- 2 tbsp. tomato paste

- 1 tsp. chili powder

Directions:

1. Toss potatoes in oil.

2. Sprinkle with salt, garlic powder, and paprika.

3. Add a crisper plate to the air fryer basket.

4. Add a basket to the Smart Grill Grill.

5. Set it to Air Fry. Set it to 360 °F for 30 minutes.

6. Press Start to preheat.

7. Put the potatoes on the crisper plate after 3 minutes.

8. Cook for 25 minutes.

9. While waiting, mix the remaining ingredients.

10. Toss potatoes in spicy mayo mixture and serve.

Nutrition: Calories: 178, Fat: 10 g, Saturated Fat: 5 g, Carbs: 39 g, Fiber: 6 g, Sodium: 29 mg, Protein: 5 g.

5. Juicy Korean Chii Pork Delight

Preparation time: 5-10 minutes

Cooking time: 8 minutes

Servings: 4

Ingredients:

- Red pepper flakes

- 3 tsp. s pepper

- 2 tbsp. sesame seeds

- 3 tbsp. Korean Red Chili Paste

- ½ cup brown Sugar:

- ½ cup of soy sauce

- 1 yellow onion, sliced

- 3 tbsp. green onion, minced

- 5 garlic cloves, minced

- 2 pounds pork, cut into 1/8 inch slices

Directions:

1. Take a re-sealable zip bag and add all of the listed ingredients

2. Zip up the bag and let it sit in your fridge for 6-8 hours

3. Pre-heat your Smart Grill Grill in Medium heat setting timer to 8 minutes

4. Arrange the sliced-up pork over your grill grate

5. Lock lid and cook for 4 minutes, flip the meat and cook for 4 minutes more

6. Serve with chopped lettuce

7. *Enjoy!*

Nutrition: Calories: 621, Fat: 31 g, Saturated Fat: 12 g, Carbs: 29 g, Fiber: 3 g, Sodium: 1428 mg, Protein: 53 g.

6. Delish Pineapple Steak

Preparation time: 5-10 minutes

Cooking time: 8 minutes

Servings: 4

Ingredients:

- Chili powder as needed

- ¼ cup cilantro leaves, chopped

- 1 tbsp. lime juice

- Salt and pepper to taste

- 1 tbsp. canola oil

- 4 fillet mignon steaks, 6-8 ounces

- 1 medium red onion, diced

- 1 jalapeno seeded and stemmed, diced

- ½ medium pineapple, cored and diced

Directions:

- Take your fillets and rub them generously with salt and pepper

- Pre-heat your Smart Grill Grill to High, set a timer to 8 minutes

- Once you hear the beep, transfer your prepared meat to the Grill Grate

- Cook until the internal temperature reaches 125 °F

- Take a bowl and add pineapple, jalapeno, onion, and mix

- Add lime juice, chili powder, coriander

- Serve the prepared fillets with the mixture with pineapple on top

- ***Enjoy!***

Nutrition: Calories: 530, Fat: 22 g, Saturated Fat: 7 g, Carbs: 21 g, Fiber: 4 g, Sodium: 286 mg, Protein: 58 g.

7. <u>Authentic Korean Flank Steak</u>

Preparation time: 10 minutes

Cooking time: 10 minutes

Servings: 4

Ingredients:

- 1 tsp. Red pepper flakes

- ½ cup and 1 tbsp. soy sauce

- 1 and ½ pounds flank steak

- ¼ cup and 2 tbsp. vegetable oil

- ½ cup of rice wine vinegar

- 3 tbsp. Sriracha

- 2 cucumbers, seeded and sliced

- 4 garlic cloves, minced

- 2 tbsp. ginger, minced

- 2 tbsp. honey

- 3 tbsp. sesame oil

- 1 tsp. Sugar:

- Salt to taste

Directions:

1. Take a bowl and add ½ cup soy sauce, half of rice wine, honey, ginger, garlic, 2 tbsp. Sriracha, 2 tbsp. sesame oil, vegetable oil

2. Mix well, pour half of the mixture over steak and rub well

3. Cover steak and let it sit for 10 minutes

4. Prepare the salad mix by adding the remaining rice wine vinegar, sesame oil, Sugar: red pepper flakes, Sriracha sauce, soy sauce, and salt to a salad bowl

5. Pre-heat your Smart Grill Grill on a High setting, with the timer set to 12 minutes

6. Transfer steak to your Grill and cook for 6 minutes per side

7. Slice and serve with the salad mix

8. *Enjoy!*

Nutrition: Calories: 327, Fat: 4 g, Saturated Fat: 0.5 g, Carbs: 33 g, Fiber: 1 g, Sodium: 142 mg, Protein: 24 g.

8. <u>Onion Touched Beef Roast</u>

Preparation time: 5-10 minutes

Cooking time: 30 minutes

Servings: 6

Ingredients:

- 2 pounds topside beef

- 2 medium onion, chopped

- 2 sticks celery, sliced

- 1 bulb garlic, peeled and crushed

- Bunch of herbs

- 1 tbsp. butter

- 3 tbsp. olive oil

- Salt and pepper to taste

Directions:

1. Add listed ingredients into a mixing bowl

2. Combine well with each other

3. Pre-heat your Smart Grill by pressing the "Roast" option and setting it to 380 °F

4. Set your timer to 30 minutes

5. Let it pre-heat until it beeps

6. Arrange bowl mixture in your Nina Foodi Pan

7. Cook for 30 minutes

8. Serve and enjoy!

Nutrition: Calories: 320, Fat: 17 g, Saturated Fat: 4 g, Carbs: 11 g, Fiber: 1.5 g, Sodium: 185 mg, Protein: 31 g.

9. Asian Pork Meal

Preparation time: 5-10 minutes

Cooking time: 25 minutes

Servings: 5

Ingredients:

- 1 pound pork ribs

- ¼ cup apple cider vinegar

- ¼ cup of soy sauce

- 1 tsp. onion powder

- 1 tsp. garlic powder

- ¼ cup hoisin sauce

Directions:

1. Take your mixing bowl and add all of the listed ingredients into the bowl

2. Combine well, add pork, and transfer to the fridge. Let it sit and chill for 3-4 hours

3. Set your Foodi Grill to "Medium" and set the timer to 24 minutes

4. Once you hear the beep, transfer the prepared pork to your grill grate, cook for 12 minutes, flip and cook for 12 minutes more

5. *Enjoy!*

Nutrition: Calories: 326, Fat: 9 g, Saturated Fat: 3 g, Carbs: 26 g, Fiber: 5 g, Sodium: 529 mg, Protein: 27 g.

10. <u>Pineapple Dump Cake</u>

Preparation time: 5 minutes

Cooking time: 3 hr. 5 minutes

Servings: 12

Ingredients:

- 14 ounces undrained canned crushed pineapple

- 1 tbsp. granulated sugar:

- 1 box yellow cake mix

- 1 cup of butter melted

Directions:

1. Add pineapple to the bottom of the greased pot.

2. Sprinkle the Sugar: on the top.

3. Then sprinkle dry cake mix on top of the cake mix.

4. Pour the melted butter slowly over the top.

5. Place a thin, clean kitchen towel between the lid and the slow cooker.

6. Cover the lid and set the valve to the vent position.

7. Cook on High for 3 hours.

Nutrition: Calories: 328, Total fats 17 g, Fiber 1 g, Carbs 42 g, Protein: 1 g.

11. Peach Dump Cake

Preparation time: 5 minutes

Cooking time: 2 hr. 15 minutes

Servings: 6

Ingredients:

- 14.5 ounces canned peach

- Box yellow cake mix

- 1 cup of butter melted

Directions:

1. Turn on your Smart Grill and grease the bottom.

2. Add canned peach with the juice.

3. Sprinkle the dry cake mixes on the top of the peach as evenly as possible.

4. Cover the lid, set it to the Vent.

5. Cook on High for 2 hours.

6. Frost with favorite frosting.

7. Enjoy!

Nutrition: Calories: 619, Total Fat: 35 g, Fiber: 0 g, Carbs: 74 g, Protein: 3 g.

12. Chocolate Pumpkin Bars

Preparation time: 15 minutes

Cooking time: 3 hours

Servings: 16

Ingredients:

For crust:

- ¾ cup unsweetened coconut, shredded

- ¼ cup cacao powder

- ½ cup raw unsalted sunflower seeds

- ¼ tsp. salt

- ¼ cup Erythritol

- 4 tbsp. butter softened

For Filling:

- 1 (29-ounces) can sugar-free pumpkin puree

- 1 cup heavy cream

- 6 organic eggs

- ½ tsp. salt

- 1 tbsp. organic vanilla extract

- 1 tbsp. pumpkin pie spice

- 1 tsp. cinnamon liquid stevia

- 1 tsp. stevia extract

Directions:

1. Line the pot of Smart Grill with a greased parchment paper

For the crust:

1. In a food processor, add all the ingredients and pulse until a fine crumbs-like mixture is formed.

2. In the pot of prepared Smart Grill, place the crust in the mixture and press to smooth the top surface.

For the filling:

1. In the bowl of a stand mixer, add all ingredients and pulse until well combined.

2. Place the filling over crust evenly.

3. Close the Smart Grill with a crisping lid and select "Slow Cooker."

4. Set on "Low" for 3 hours.

5. Press "Start /Stop" to begin cooking.

6. With the help of parchment paper, carefully lift the bars and transfer them onto a wire rack to cool completely.

7. Cut into desired-sized bras and serve.

Nutrition: Calories: 121, Fat: 9.7 g, Carbs: 6.3 g, Fiber: 2.4 g, Sugar: 2.2 g, Proteins: 3.5 g.

13. **Easy Blueberry Cobbler**

Preparation time: 10 minutes

Cooking time: 1 Hour 5 minutes

Servings: 8

Ingredients:

- 1 cup of self-rising flour

- 1 cup of milk

- ½ cup of butter

- 1 cup of white sugar:

- 4 cups of fresh blueberries

Directions:

1. Preheat your oven to 350 °F (175 °C) and put butter to use in an 8-inches square baking dish 2. Then, melt the butter in the preheating oven for like 5 minutes and then remove it from the oven.

2. Mix sugar, flour, and milk in a bowl until they all combine. Then pour the batter over the melted butter and scatter the blueberries over the batter.

3. Bake in the already preheated oven until you insert a toothpick at the center, and it comes out clean in approximately 1 hour.

Nutrition: Calories: 310.4, Carbs: 48.5 g, Protein: 3.2 g, Fat: 12.5 g, Cholesterol 32.9 mg, Sodium: 293.4 mg.

14. <u>Cauliflower Steaks - Roasted</u>

Preparation time: 10 minutes

Cooking time: 30 minutes

Servings: 4

Ingredients:

- 1 pinch of red pepper flakes

- 1 tbsp. of lemon juice (fresh)

- ¼ cup of olive oil

- 2 cloves of garlic, minced

- 1 pinch of salt and ground black pepper

- 1 cauliflower (large head) sliced vertically into four.

Directions:

1. Preheat the oven to 400 °F (200 °C). Get parchment paper to line your baking sheet.

2. Put cauliflower steaks on the already prepared sheet.

3. Whisk lemon juice, olive oil, red pepper flakes, garlic, black pepper, and salt inside a small bowl. Then, apply about half the olive oil quantity you have already mixed on the cauliflower steaks.

4. Then, in the already preheated oven, you will need to put the cauliflower steaks and roast them for about 15 minutes. Each steak should be turned to the other side, and you will then apply the leftover olive oil on it as you did earlier. You will need to roast for about 15-20 minutes when the steaks become tender with golden color.

Nutrition: Calories: 175.8, Carbs: 12.1 g, Protein: 4.3 g, Fat 13.8 g, Sodium: 63.6 mg.

15. <u>Grilled Pineapple Butterscotch Sundaes</u>

Preparation time: 10 minutes

Cooking time: 25 minutes

Servings: 12

Ingredients:

- 2 tbsp. of white sugar

- 2 each of fresh pineapples, to be peeled, cored, and cut into 6 spears

- 1 cup of packed brown sugar:

- 6 tbsp. of butter

- ¼ tsp. of ground nutmeg

- ½ cup of butter

- ½ cup of heavy whipping cream

- 1 pinch of salt

- 1 tsp. vanilla extract

- 3 cups of vanilla ice cream

Directions:

1. Preheat the grill with medium heat and lightly oil the grate 2. Heat 6 tbsp. Of butter, nutmeg, and white Sugar: in a saucepan on medium heat and stir until the Sugar: dissolves in about 5 minutes. Then brush the pineapple spears with butter mixture.

2. Arrange pineapple on the already preheated grill and cover, grill until it becomes lightly brown, turning frequently; this should last between 7 to 10 minutes. Then transfer the pineapple to a platter.

3. Get another saucepan and melt the remaining ½ cup of butter using medium heat. Stir in heavy cream and brown sugar, then bring to a boil, stirring as frequently as possible. Remove from the heat and add salt and vanilla extract. Serve the pineapple topped with ice cream and cream sauce.

Nutrition: Calories: 388.2, Carbs: 51.9 g, Protein: 2.7 g, Fat: 21 g, Cholesterol: 63.7 mg, Sodium: 131.2 mg.

16. <u>Glazed Carrots</u>

Preparation time: 10 minutes

Cooking time: 15 minutes

Servings: 8

Ingredients:

- ¼ cup of butter

- ¼ tsp. of salt

- 2 pounds of carrots should be peeled and cut into steaks

- ¼ cup of packed brown sugar:

- 1 /8 tsp. of ground white pepper

Directions:

1. Place the carrots into a large saucepan, pour water to reach 1-inch depth, and bring to a boil. Reduce the heat to low, cover, and simmer the carrots until they become tender in about 8-10 minutes. Drain and transfer to a neat bowl.

2. Melt butter in the same saucepan, stir salt, brown sugar, and white pepper into the butter until the salt and Sugar: have dissolved. Transfer the carrots into brown Sugar: sauce; cook and keep stirring until the carrots are glazed with the sauce in about 5 minutes.

Nutrition: Calories: 123.6, Carbs: 17.6 g, Protein: 1.1 g, Fat 6 g, Cholesterol 15.3 mg, Sodium: 193.8 mg.

17. <u>Delicious Cajun Eggplant</u>

Preparation time: 5-10 minutes

Cooking time: 12 minutes

Servings: 4

Ingredients:

- ¼ cup olive oil

- 2 small eggplants, cut into slices

- 3 tsp. Cajun seasoning

- 2 tbsp. lime juice

Directions:

1. Coat eggplant slices with oil, lemon juice, and Cajun seasoning

2. Take your Smart Grill Grill and press "Grill," and set to "Medium" mode; set the timer to 10 minutes

3. Let it preheat

4. Arrange eggplants over grill grate, lock lid, and cook for 5 minutes

5. Flip and cook for 5 minutes more

6. Serve and enjoy!

Nutrition: Calories: 362, Fat: 11 g, Saturated Fat: 3 g, Carbs: 16 g, Fiber: 1 g, Sodium: 694 mg, Protein: 8 g.

18. Cool Rosemary Potatoes

Preparation time: 10 minutes

Cooking time: 20 minutes

Servings: 4

Ingredients:

- 2 pounds baby red potatoes, quartered

- ½ tsp. Parsley, dried

- ¼ tsp. celery powder

- 2 tbsp. Extra virgin olive oil

- ¼ cup onion flakes, dried

- ½ tsp. Garlic powder

- ½ tsp. Onion powder

- ½ tsp. Salt

- ¼ tsp. freshly ground black pepper

Directions:

1. Add all listed ingredients into a large bowl

2. Toss well and coat them well

3. Preheat your Smart Grill by pressing the "Air Crisp" option and setting it to 390 °F

4. Set the timer to 20 minutes

5. Allow it to preheat until it beeps

6. Once preheated, add potatoes to the cooking basket

7. Close the lid and cook for 10 minutes

8. Shake the basket and cook for 10 minutes more

9. Check the crispness if it is done or not

10. Cook for 5 minutes more if needed

11. Serve and enjoy!

Nutrition: Calories: 232, Fat: 7 g, Saturated Fat: 1 g, Carbs: 39 g, Fiber: 6 g, Sodium: 249 mg, Protein: 4 g.

19. <u>Cheesy Broccoli Quiche</u>

Preparation time: 40 minutes

Cooking time: 45 minutes

Servings: 2

Ingredients:

- 1 cup of water

- 2 cups broccoli florets

- 1 carrot, chopped

- 1 cup cheddar cheese, grated

- 1/4 cup Feta cheese, crumbled

- 1/4 cup milk

- 2 eggs

- 1 tsp. parsley

- 1 tsp. thyme

- Salt and pepper to taste

Directions:

1. Pour the water inside. Place the basket inside.

2. Put the carrots and broccoli on the basket. Cover the pot.

3. Set it to pressure. Cook at high pressure for 2 minutes.

4. Release the pressure quickly. Crack the eggs into a bowl and beat.

5. Season with salt, pepper, parsley, and thyme. Put the vegetables on a small baking pan. Layer with the cheese and pour in the beaten eggs Place on the basket.

6. Choose Air Crisp function. Seal the crisping lid. Cook at 350 °For 20 minutes.

Nutrition: Calories: 400, Total Fat: 28 g, Saturated Fat 16.5 g, Cholesterol 242 mg, Sodium: 688 mg, Total Carbs: 12.8 g, Dietary Fiber 3.3 g, Total Sugar: 5.8 g, Protein: 26.2 g, Potassium: 537 mg.

20. **Italian Spiced Squash**

Preparation time: 5-10 minutes

Cooking time: 16 minutes

Servings: 4

Ingredients:

- ¼ tsp. black pepper

- 1 ½ tsp. dried oregano

- 1 tbsp. Olive oil

- ½ tsp. salt

- 1 tsp. dried thyme

- 1 medium butternut squash, peeled and seeded, cut into ½ inch slices

Directions:

1. Take a mixing bowl and add listed ingredients alongside the slices, mix

2. Pre-heat your Smart Grill Grill to Medium, setting the timer to 16 minutes

3. Once you hear the beep, arrange squash over the griller

4. Cook for 8 minutes, flip them over and cook for 8 minutes more

5. Serve and enjoy once done!

Nutrition: Calories: 238, Fat: 12 g, Saturated Fat: 2 g, Carbs: 36 g, Fiber: 3 g, Sodium: 128 mg, Protein: 15 g.

21. Ranch Flavored Cauliflower Steak

Preparation time: 10 minutes

Cooking time: 15 minutes

Servings: 4

Ingredients:

- 1 head cauliflower, stemmed and leaves removed

- ¼ cup canola oil

- ½ tsp. garlic powder

- ½ tsp. paprika

- Salt and pepper to taste

- 1 cup cheddar cheese, shredded

- Ranch dressing, garnish

- 4 slices bacon, cooked and crumbled

- 2 tbsp. chopped fresh chives

Directions:

1. Cut cauliflower from top to bottom into 2-inches steaks, reserve the remaining cauliflower to cook

2. Take a small-sized bowl and whisk in oil, garlic powder, paprika, season with salt and pepper

3. Brush each steak with oil mixture on both sides

4. Preheat Smart Grill by pressing the "Grill" option and setting it to "Maximum" and timer to 15 minutes

5. Let it preheat until you hear a beep

6. Transfer steaks to Grill Grate, lock lid, and grill for 10 minutes

7. After 10 minutes, flip steaks and top with ½ cup cheese

8. Lock lid and cook for 5 minutes more

9. Once done, drizzle with ranch dressing, top with bacon and chives

10. *Enjoy!*

Nutrition: Calories: 720, Fat: 19 g, Saturated Fat: 19 g, Carbs: 11 g, Fiber: 4 g, Sodium: 1555 mg, Protein: 32 g.

Lightning Source UK Ltd.
Milton Keynes UK
UKHW020758110621
385329UK00001B/225